Editor
Eric Migliaccio

Editor in Chief
Ina Massler Levin, M.A.

Creative Director
Karen J. Goldfluss, M.S. Ed.

Illustrator
Renée Mc Elwee

Cover Artist
Brenda DiAntonis

Art Coordinator
Renée Mc Elwee

Imaging
Rosa C. See
Craig Gunnell

Publisher

Mary D. Smith, M.S. Ed.

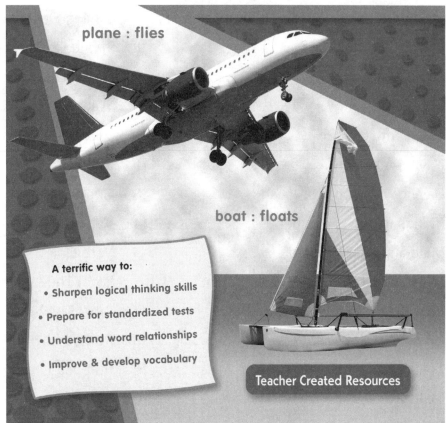

plane : flies

boat : floats

A terrific way to:

• Sharpen logical thinking skills

• Prepare for standardized tests

• Understand word relationships

• Improve & develop vocabulary

Teacher Created Resources

TCR 3165

Author

Ruth Foster, M.Ed.

Teacher Created Resources
6421 Industry Way
Westminster, CA 92683
www.teachercreated.com
ISBN: 978-1-4206-3165-4
© 2011 Teacher Created Resources
Made in U.S.A.

Teacher Created Resources

Table of Contents

Introduction

Think of an analogy as a wonderful puzzle, and one has a great interdisciplinary teaching exercise.

An analogy is a type of comparison. An analogy is when a likeness is found between two unlike things. If approached as a puzzle, one solves the analogy by finding out how the pieces fit together. What links the words to each other? How can they be connected or tied together? What is the relationship between them?

> **cat** is to **meow** as **dog** is to __***bark***__

Although the example above may appear to be easy, it is an exercise that involves cognitive processes and critical-thinking skills. One must comprehend the words read, categorize them, understand the connection between them, and then find a similar connection between a different pair of words. In this case, both *meow* and *bark* are sounds that a cat and dog make, respectively.

Analogies written for this series will focus on a variety of word relationships. They will develop, reinforce, and expand skills in the following areas:

→ visual imagery
→ reading comprehension
→ paying attention to detail (word sequence within word pairs)
→ vocabulary development
→ synonym, antonym, and homophone recognition and recall
→ understanding different shades of word meanings
→ reasoning
→ standardized-test taking

Students will be able to demonstrate mastery by doing the following:

→ working with both multiple-choice and write-out question formats
→ analyzing and fixing incorrect analogies
→ writing their own analogies in both question and sentence format

For interdisciplinary practice, some analogies will be subject-specific (addressing science, math, or social studies, for example). Others will push students to think outside of the box, as creative and imaginative connections between words will be asked for. Students may then explain in writing or verbally (depending on skill level) how they created analogous word pairs or situations.

Blank answer sheets can be found on page 61. Use these sheets to provide your students with practice in answering questions in a standardized-test format.

Fitting Pictures Together

Directions: Look at the pictures below. One of the pictures does not fit in with the others. Cross out the one that does not fit in.

1.

2.

3.

4.

5.

6.

Tell or Write: Pick one of the questions above. Tell or write why the picture didn't fit in.

Fitting Pictures Together 2

Directions: Look at the pictures below. One of the pictures does not fit in with the others. Cross out the one that does not fit in.

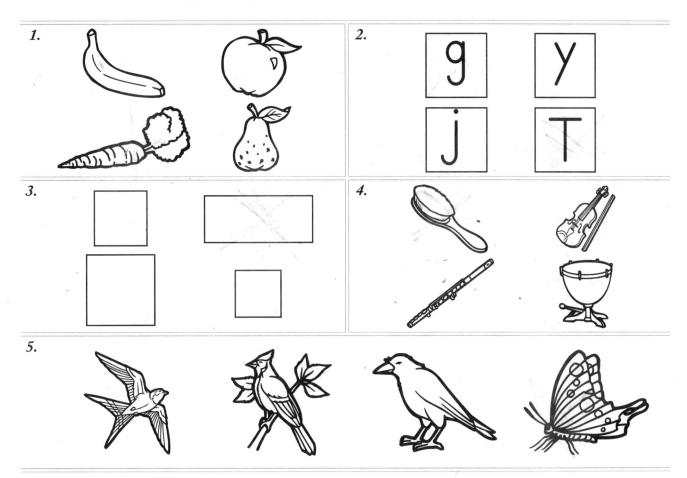

Directions: Draw four pictures, shapes, or letters. One of the pictures should not fit in.

Tell or Write: Which one of your pictures did not fit in? Explain why.

_____

- -

_____

- -

_____

Fitting Pictures Together 3

Directions: Look at the pictures below. One of the pictures does not fit in with the others. Cross out the one that does not fit in.

1.

2.

3.

4.

5.

6.

Tell or Write: Pick one question. Tell or write why the picture didn't fit in.

Linking Pictures

Directions: Look at each row of pictures. Which picture can best be linked with the first picture? Fill in the correct bubble.

Tell or Write: Pick one question. Tell or write how the picture you chose can be linked to the first picture.

_____

- -

_____

- -

_____

Linking Pictures 2

Directions: Look at each row of pictures. Which picture can best be linked with the first picture? Fill in the correct bubble.

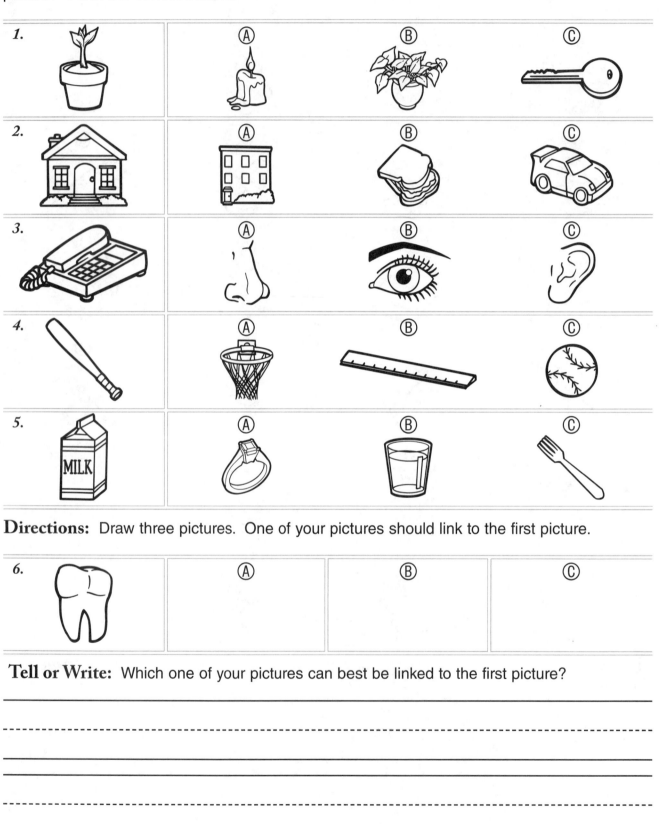

Directions: Draw three pictures. One of your pictures should link to the first picture.

Tell or Write: Which one of your pictures can best be linked to the first picture?

_____

- -

_____

- -

_____

Linking Pictures 3

Directions: Look at each row of pictures. Which picture can best be linked with the first picture? Fill in the correct bubble.

Tell or Write: Pick one question. Tell or write how the picture you chose can be linked to the first picture.

_____

- -

_____

_____

- -

_____

The Same Link

Directions: Look at these pictures to the right.
Think about how these two things are linked.

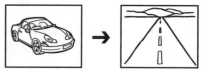

Now choose the answer that will link to each first picture in the same way.

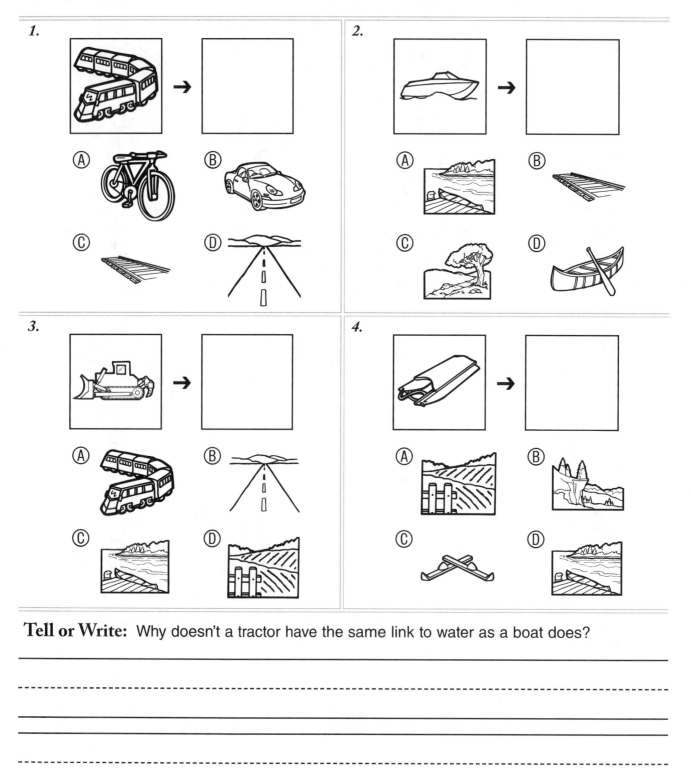

Tell or Write: Why doesn't a tractor have the same link to water as a boat does?

_____

- -

_____

_____

- -

_____

The Same Link 2

Directions: Look at these pictures to the right.
Think about how these two things are linked.

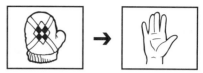

Now choose the answer that will link to each first picture in the same way.

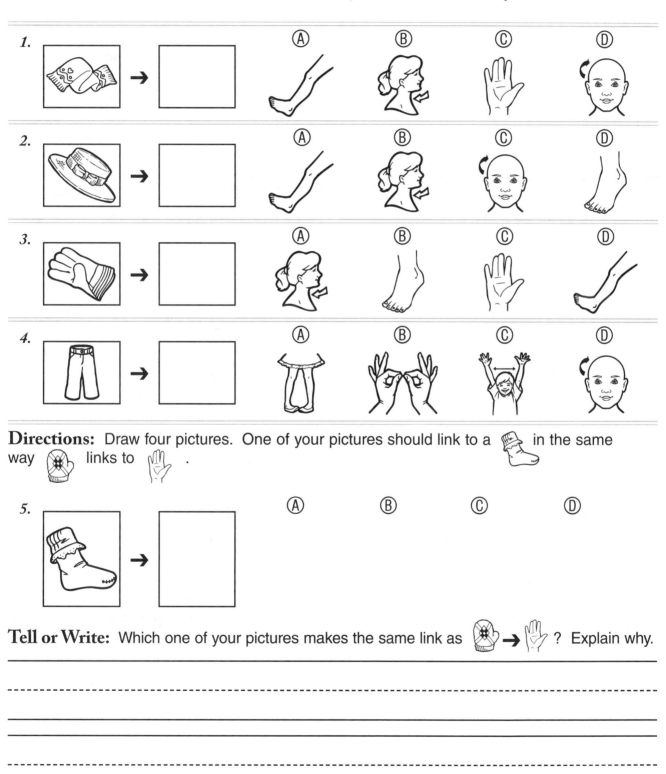

Directions: Draw four pictures. One of your pictures should link to a 🧦 in the same way 🧤 links to 🖐 .

5.

Ⓐ   Ⓑ   Ⓒ   Ⓓ

Tell or Write: Which one of your pictures makes the same link as 🧤 → 🖐 ? Explain why.

_____

- -

_____

_____

- -

_____

Paying Attention

Directions: Look at each row of pictures. Which picture can best be linked with the first picture? Fill in the correct bubble.

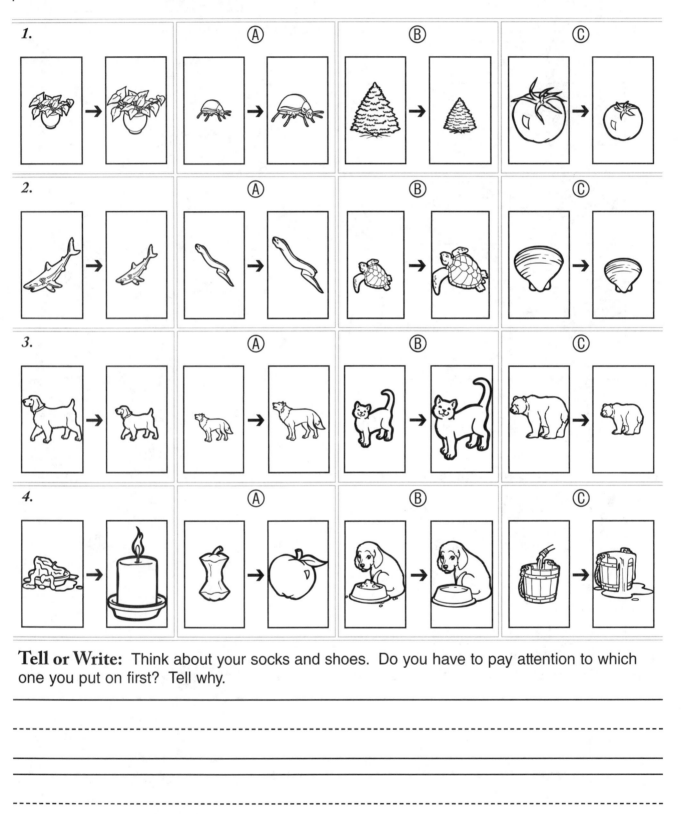

Tell or Write: Think about your socks and shoes. Do you have to pay attention to which one you put on first? Tell why.

_____

- -

_____

- -

_____

Paying Attention 2

Directions: Look at the pictures in the first pair. Think about how they are linked. Find the pair that is linked in the same way. Pay attention to what comes first and second!

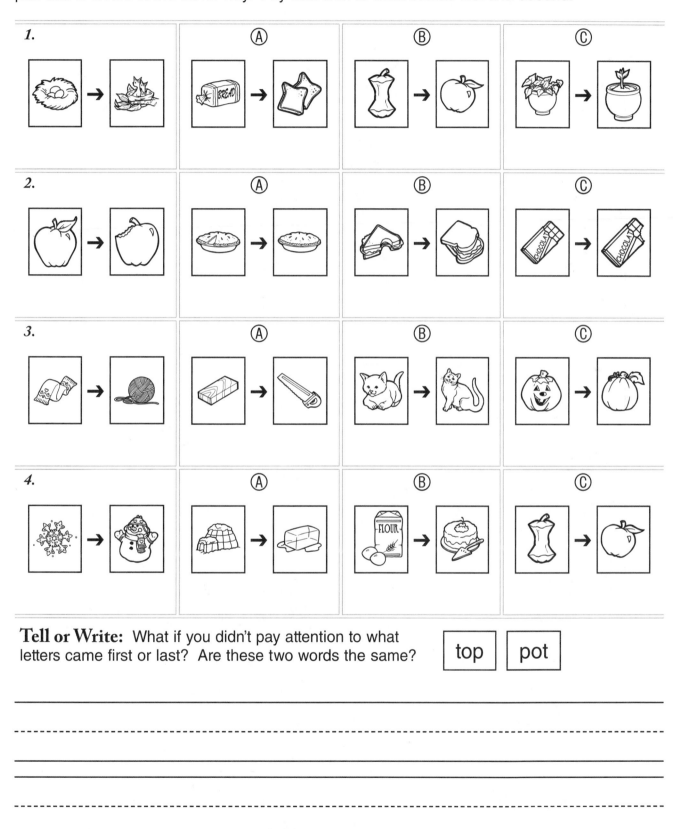

Tell or Write: What if you didn't pay attention to what letters came first or last? Are these two words the same? | top | pot |

Things that Go Together

Directions: We tend to think of some words in pairs. When we think of one, we think of the other, too. See if you find the picture that completes the pair.

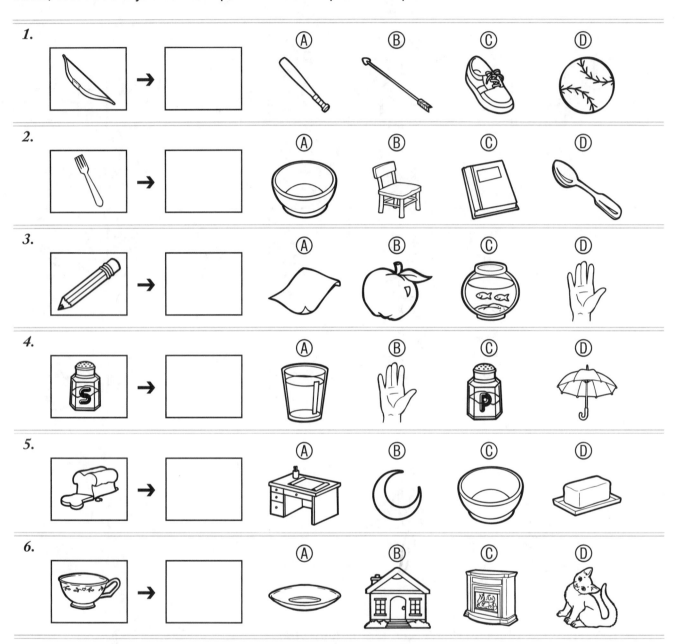

Tell or Write: What one thing do these two things make you think of?

- chalk + eraser = _____

_____

- match + wood = _____

_____

Matching Linking Pairs

Directions: Make a copy of this page. Cut out the pictures. Match the pictures to make four sets of linking pairs. Glue the pairs on another piece of paper.

Matching Linking Pairs 2

Directions: Make a copy of this page. Cut out the pictures. Match the pictures to make four sets of linking pairs. Glue the pairs on another piece of paper.

Body Parts

Directions: Look at how the pictures in the first box are linked. Find the answer that links to the thing in the second box in the same way.

1.

A   B   C

1   2   3

2.

A   B   C

3.

A   B   C

6   10   20

4.

A   B   C

Directions: Write answers for this question. Only one of your answers should be correct.

5.

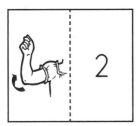 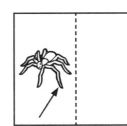

Ⓐ _____

Ⓑ _____

Ⓒ _____

Tell or Write: Which one of your answers for question 5 was correct? Tell why.

_____

_____

_____

Color

Directions: Use your crayons to color in the boxes. (You can do this with your teacher or by yourself.) This will help you remember your color words.

red	blue	yellow	orange	black	green	brown

Look at how the pictures in the first box are linked. Find the answer that links to the thing in the second box in the same way.

1.

yellow

Ⓐ red

Ⓑ yellow

Ⓒ blue

2.

green

Ⓐ pink

Ⓑ black

Ⓒ green

3.

orange

red

Ⓐ

Ⓑ

Ⓒ

4.

yellow

Ⓐ orange

Ⓑ brown

Ⓒ green

Directions: Write answers for this question. Make sure only one answer is correct.

5.

purple

STOP

Ⓐ _____   Ⓑ _____   Ⓒ _____

Tell or Write: Which of your answers was correct? Explain why.

_____

_____

_____

_____

Math

Directions: Find the answer that links to the first pair in the same way.

1. ⬤ is to ◐ as ▭ is to
   - Ⓐ ◐ (circle, half shaded)
   - Ⓑ ▭ (rectangle, right half shaded)
   - Ⓒ ☐ (empty square)

2. △ is to ◭ as ▯ is to
   - Ⓐ ▪ (square, top shaded)
   - Ⓑ ▭ (rectangle, right half shaded)
   - Ⓒ ▯ (rectangle, right half shaded)

3. △ is to 3 as ☐ is to
   - Ⓐ 2
   - Ⓑ 3
   - Ⓒ 4

4. ⯃ is to 8 as ⬠ is to
   - Ⓐ 5
   - Ⓑ 6
   - Ⓒ 7

5. ⬆ is to ⬇ as △ is to
   - Ⓐ ◁
   - Ⓑ ▽
   - Ⓒ ▷

6. 𝍸 is to 6 as 𝍷𝍷 is to
   - Ⓐ 9
   - Ⓑ 11
   - Ⓒ 13

Tell or Write: Many students think question 2 is very hard. Did you? Why or why not?

_____

- -

_____

_____

- -

_____

Math 2

Directions: Find the answer that links to the first pair in the same way.

1.

 is to (circle quartered) as (shaded rectangle) is to

(A)   (C)

(B) (square with bottom-left shaded)

2.

 is to 3 as is to

(A) 2   (C) 4

(B) 3

3.

1 is to 3 as 5 is to

(A) 6   (C) 8

(B) 7

4.

 is to $\dfrac{2}{5}$ as is to

(A) $\dfrac{5}{4}$ (C) $\dfrac{4}{5}$

(B) $\dfrac{3}{5}$

Directions: Make your own answers. Only one answer should be correct.

5.

9 is to 8 as 4 is to

(A) _____   (C) _____

(B) _____

Tell or Write: Which one of your answers for question 5 was correct? Tell or write why.

_____

_____

_____

Math 3

Directions: Look at the Set 1 pictures. Think about how they are linked. Choose the answer that will link to the pictures in the same way.

Set 1

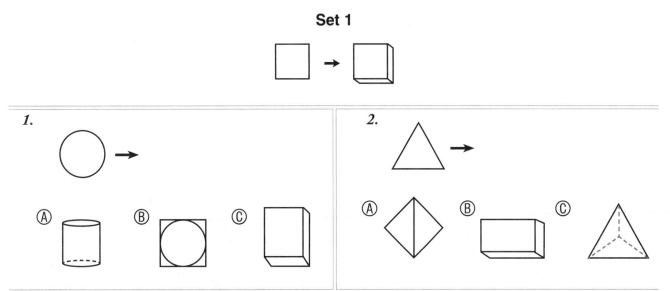

Directions: Look at the Set 2 pictures. Think about how they are linked. Choose the answer that will link to the pictures in the same way.

Set 2

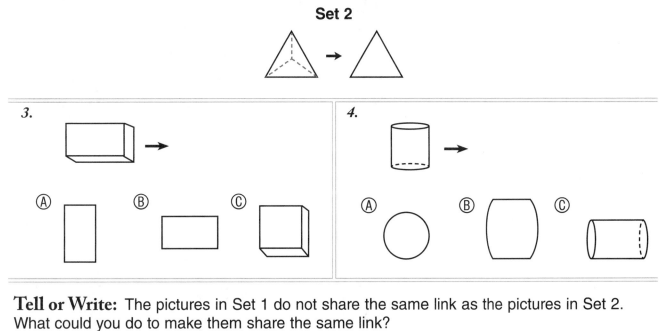

Tell or Write: The pictures in Set 1 do not share the same link as the pictures in Set 2. What could you do to make them share the same link?

_____

- -

_____

_____

- -

_____

Social Studies

Directions: Use the map to help you pick the answer that has the same link as the two pictures in the first box.

1.   is to as is to

    Ⓐ   Ⓒ

    Ⓑ

2.   is to as is to

    Ⓐ   Ⓒ

    Ⓑ

3. S is to as N is to

    Ⓐ   Ⓒ

    Ⓑ

4.   is to as W is to

    Ⓐ S   Ⓒ N

    Ⓑ E

5.   is to N as is to

    Ⓐ S   Ⓒ

    Ⓑ N

Social Studies 2

Directions: Use the compass and the map of the continental United States to help you answer the questions.

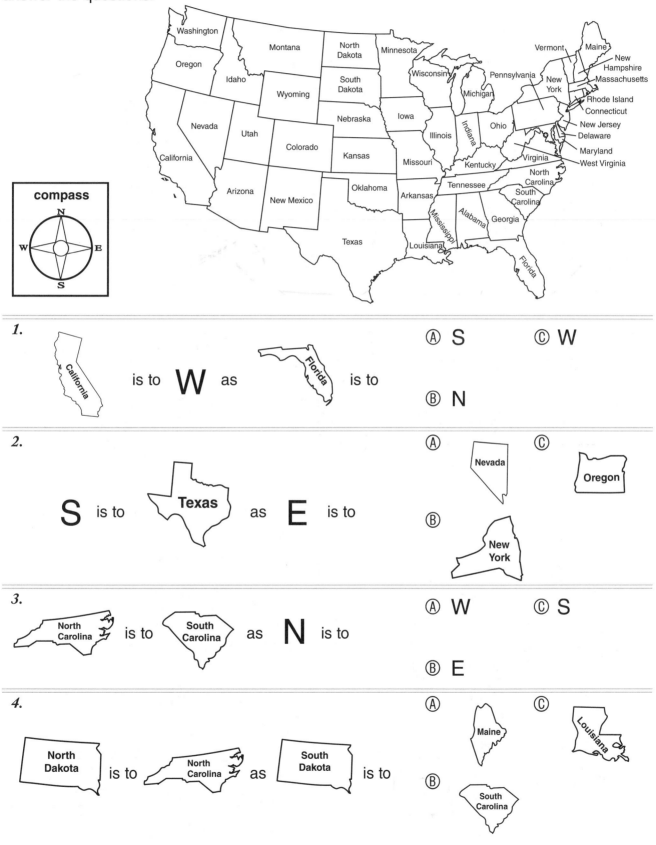

1. California is to **W** as Florida is to

   Ⓐ S   Ⓒ W
   Ⓑ N

2. **S** is to Texas as **E** is to

   Ⓐ Nevada   Ⓒ Oregon
   Ⓑ New York

3. North Carolina is to South Carolina as **N** is to

   Ⓐ W   Ⓒ S
   Ⓑ E

4. North Dakota is to North Carolina as South Dakota is to

   Ⓐ Maine   Ⓒ Louisiana
   Ⓑ South Carolina

Time

Directions: Find the answer that links to the first pair in the same way.

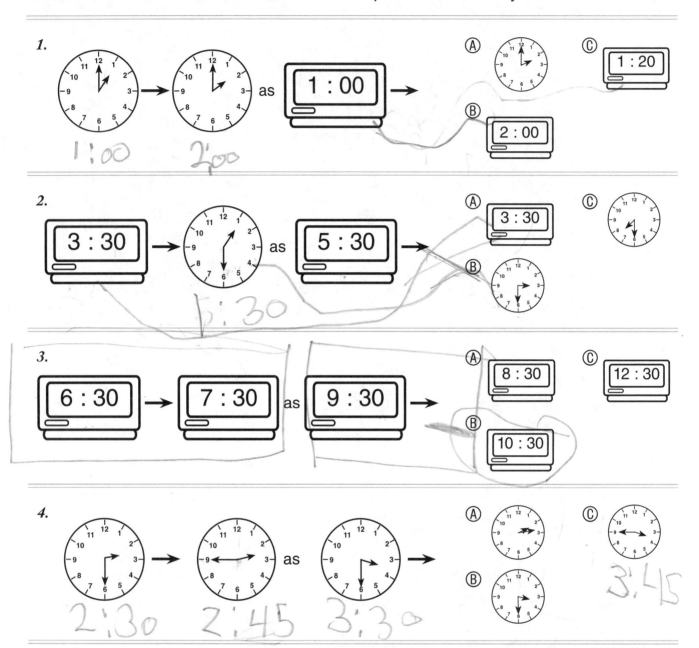

1.

as

1 : 00

Ⓐ

Ⓒ 1 : 20

Ⓑ 2 : 00

1:00   2:00

2.

3 : 30

as

5 : 30

Ⓐ 3 : 30

Ⓒ

Ⓑ

5:30

3.

6 : 30 → 7 : 30 as 9 : 30

Ⓐ 8 : 30

Ⓒ 12 : 30

Ⓑ 10 : 30

4.

as

Ⓐ

Ⓒ

Ⓑ

2:30   2:45   3:30   3:45

Tell or Write: Write down when your school day starts and ends. Add numbers to each digital clock. Add hands to each round clock.

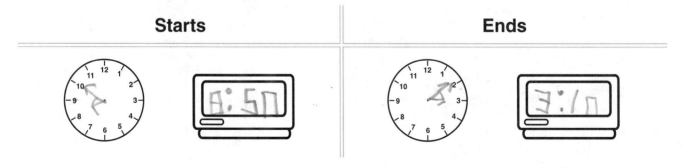

Starts	Ends

Time 2

Directions: Find the answer that links to the first pair in the same way.

> **Facts to Help**
> • **A.M.** or **a.m.** is the time from **midnight** to just before **noon.**
> • **P.M.** or **p.m.** is the time from **noon** to just before **midnight.**

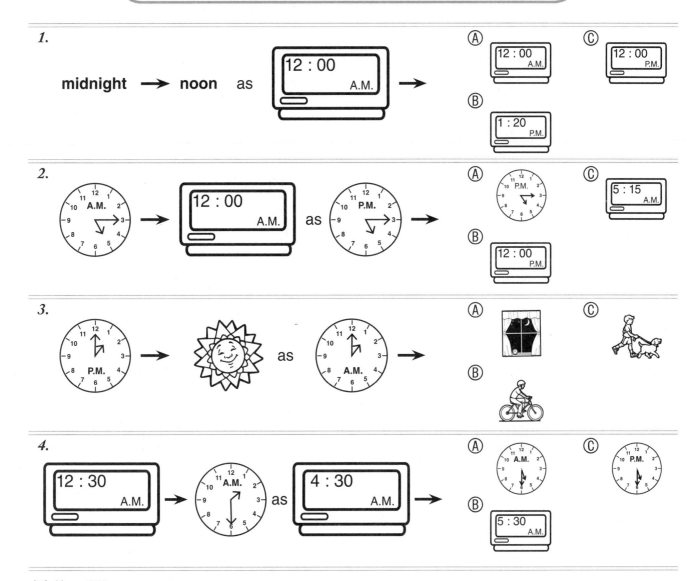

Tell or Write: If you are meeting someone at 7:00, why is it important to let that person know if you mean 7:00 a.m. or 7:00 p.m.?

_____

- -

_____

_____

- -

_____

Science

Directions: Look at the pictures in the first box. Think about how they are linked. Choose the answer that will link to the pictures in the same way.

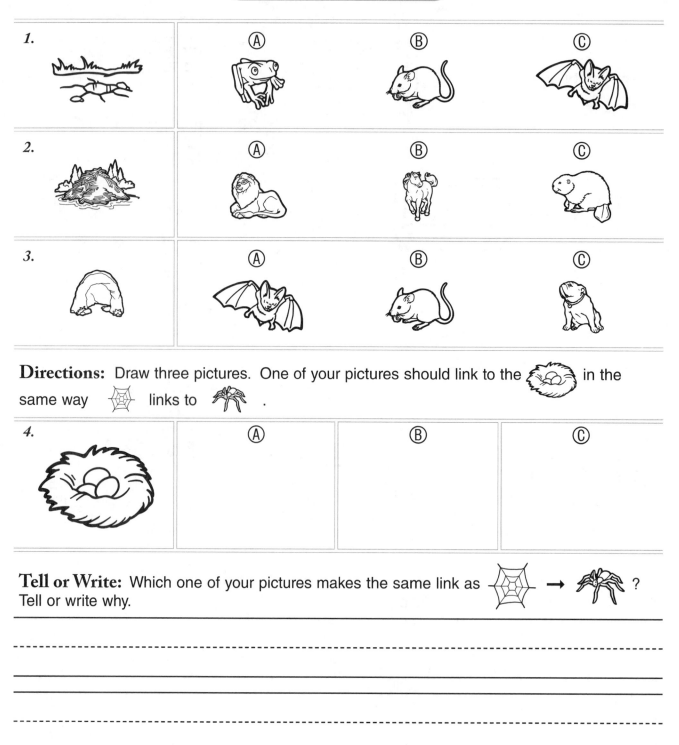

Directions: Draw three pictures. One of your pictures should link to the 🪺 in the same way 🕸 links to 🕷 .

Tell or Write: Which one of your pictures makes the same link as 🕸 → 🕷 ? Tell or write why.

_____

- -

_____

_____

- -

_____

Science 2

Directions: Find the answer that links to the first pair in the same way.

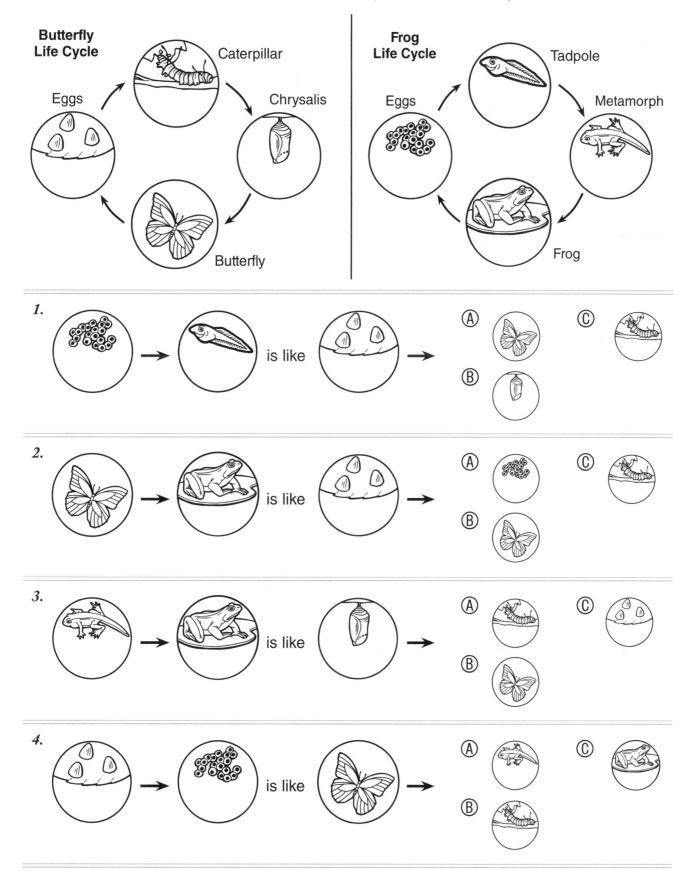

The Solar System

Directions: Use the picture of our solar system to help you find the word that best completes the pair.

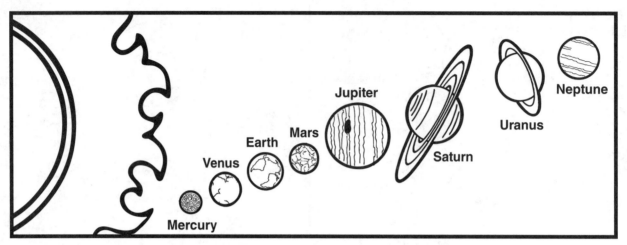

1. **Mercury** is to **Earth** as **Earth** is to
   - (A) Mars
   - (B) Venus
   - (C) Jupiter
   - (D) Neptune

2. **Neptune** is to **Uranus** as **Jupiter** is to
   - (A) Venus
   - (B) Mars
   - (C) Saturn
   - (D) Earth

3. **Earth** is to **3** as **Jupiter** is to
   - (A) 3
   - (B) 5
   - (C) 7
   - (D) 9

4. **4** is to **6** as **Mars** is to
   - (A) Uranus
   - (B) Neptune
   - (C) Venus
   - (D) Saturn

5. **biggest** is to **smallest** as **Jupiter** is to
   - (A) Mercury
   - (B) Venus
   - (C) Earth
   - (D) Saturn

Tell or Write: Which planet do you live on?

Keep this page! You will need to use the picture of the solar system again.

The Solar System 2

Directions: The moon chart shows how many moons each planet has. Use the moon chart to help you find the word that best completes the pair. You may want to look at the picture of the solar system used in the lesson before (page 28).

Moon Chart

Planet	Mercury	Venus	Earth	Mars	Jupiter	Saturn	Uranus	Neptune
Number of Moons	0	0	1	2	62	33	27	13

1. **Saturn** is to **33** as **Uranus** is to

   Ⓐ 0   Ⓑ 62   Ⓒ 13   Ⓓ 27

2. **0** is to **1** as **Venus** is to

   Ⓐ Neptune   Ⓑ Mercury   Ⓒ Mars   Ⓓ Earth

3. **biggest planet** is to **62** as **smallest planet** is to

   Ⓐ 0   Ⓑ 1   Ⓒ 2   Ⓓ 13

4. **Sun** is to **Earth** as **Earth** is to

   Ⓐ Venus   Ⓑ Jupiter   Ⓒ moon   Ⓓ planet

5. **closest to the sun** is to **0** as **farthest from the sun** is to

   Ⓐ 1   Ⓑ 13   Ⓒ 33   Ⓓ 62

Tell or Write: Do the biggest planets have the most moons?

_____

_____

_____

_____

_____

Antonyms

Directions: Find word pairs that share the same link.

> **hot** is to **cold** as . . .

1. **big** is to

   Ⓐ large   Ⓑ funny   Ⓒ small

2. **sad** is to

   Ⓐ bad   Ⓑ happy   Ⓒ silly

3. **tall** is to

   Ⓐ short   Ⓑ big   Ⓒ good

4. **old** is to

   Ⓐ young   Ⓑ large   Ⓒ small

5. **awake** is to

   Ⓐ silly   Ⓑ big   Ⓒ asleep

6. **many** is to

   Ⓐ lots   Ⓑ few   Ⓒ small

7. **over** is to

   Ⓐ top   Ⓑ young   Ⓒ under

8. **in** is to

   Ⓐ out   Ⓑ asleep   Ⓒ near

9. **slow** is to

   Ⓐ few   Ⓑ happy   Ⓒ fast

10. **near** is to

    Ⓐ funny   Ⓑ far   Ⓒ lots

Tell or Write: An *antonym* is a word that is opposite in meaning to another word. Were your answers antonyms? Tell why or why not.

_____

- -

_____

_____

- -

_____

Synonyms

Directions: Find word pairs that share the same link.

> **glad** is to **happy** as . . .

1. **small** is to

   Ⓐ big   Ⓑ tiny   Ⓒ quick

2. **big** is to

   Ⓐ little   Ⓑ silly   Ⓒ large

3. **trap** is to

   Ⓐ catch   Ⓑ exit   Ⓒ yell

4. **smile** is to

   Ⓐ grin   Ⓑ shut   Ⓒ fast

5. **fast** is to

   Ⓐ wild   Ⓑ slow   Ⓒ quick

6. **cry** is to

   Ⓐ grin   Ⓑ weep   Ⓒ shout

7. **yell** is to

   Ⓐ quick   Ⓑ shout   Ⓒ wild

8. **leave** is to

   Ⓐ small   Ⓑ open   Ⓒ exit

9. **shut** is to

   Ⓐ close   Ⓑ grin   Ⓒ quick

10. **silly** is to

   Ⓐ tiny   Ⓑ leave   Ⓒ funny

Tell or Write: A *synonym* is a word that is nearly the same in meaning as another word. Were your answers synonyms? Tell why or why not.

Antonym and Synonym Practice

- *Antonyms* are words that are opposite in meaning.
- *Synonyms* are words that mean the same.

Directions: Think about the link between the first pair of words. Choose the answer for the pair of words that are linked in the same way.

- Write **A** on the line if the words are **<u>antonyms</u>**.
- Write **S** on the line if the words are **<u>synonyms</u>**.

1. **off : on**

    Ⓐ jump : rope   Ⓒ swing : bat

    Ⓑ old : new   Ⓓ go : leave

_____

2. **night : day**

    Ⓐ watch : TV   Ⓒ rest : nap

    Ⓑ listen : radio   Ⓓ early : late

_____

3. **look : watch**

    Ⓐ silly : good   Ⓒ work : job

    Ⓑ neat : messy   Ⓓ soup : bowl

_____

4. **help : hurt**

    Ⓐ sink : rise   Ⓒ many : lots

    Ⓑ sun : heat   Ⓓ play : ground

_____

5. **touch : feel**

    Ⓐ water : drink   Ⓒ house : roof

    Ⓑ close : near   Ⓓ rainy : sunny

_____

6. **loud : noisy**

    Ⓐ rich : poor   Ⓒ black : white

    Ⓑ ugly : pretty   Ⓓ fright : scare

_____

Words that Sound the Same

A word that sounds the same as another word but means something different is called a *homophone*.

Example: The words *rain* and *rein* are **homophones**.

- **Rain** is water that falls from the sky.
- A **rein** is used to guide a horse.

Directions: Find the word that best completes the pair.

---

1. **be** is to **bee** as **too** is to

Ⓐ toe   Ⓑ two   Ⓒ tan   Ⓓ tow

Now circle the words above that match these pictures:

---

2. **night** is to **knight** as **tail** is to

Ⓐ tail   Ⓑ nail   Ⓒ kale   Ⓓ tale

Now circle the words above that match these pictures:

---

3. **eight** is to **ate** as **hare** is to

Ⓐ hair   Ⓑ halt   Ⓒ hard   Ⓓ hear

Now circle the words above that match these pictures:

---

4. **flour** is to **flower** as **rode** is to

Ⓐ four   Ⓑ rower   Ⓒ road   Ⓓ raid

Now circle the words above that match these pictures:

Tell or Write: Were all of your answers homophones? Tell why or why not.

_____

_____

_____

_____

_____

Alphabet Practice

Directions: Find the answer that links to the first pair in the same way.

> **Facts to Help**
> - There are 26 letters in the alphabet.
> - Each letter has an uppercase and a lowercase form.

1. A → a

    Ⓐ C → c   Ⓑ a → A   Ⓒ b → b   Ⓓ x → X

2. 5 → E **(Hint:** Cross out answers where the number isn't first!)

    Ⓐ 10 → j   Ⓑ O → 15   Ⓒ 20 → T   Ⓓ Y → 25

3. O → N

    Ⓐ Y → Z   Ⓑ f → E   Ⓒ b → a   Ⓓ U → T

4. G → I

    Ⓐ J → K   Ⓑ L → N   Ⓒ q → s   Ⓓ W → U

5. c → D

    Ⓐ e → D   Ⓑ G → h   Ⓒ D → e   Ⓓ x → Y

6. 13 → m

    Ⓐ 4 → c   Ⓑ n → 14   Ⓒ 14 → n   Ⓓ 7 → f

Tell or Write: Which one of these letter groups would you most likely start a sentence with? Circle your answer.

> the   The   eht   ehT

Alphabet Practice 2

Directions: Find the answer that links to the first pair in the same way.

> ### Facts to Help
> - Letters in the alphabet are either vowels or consonants.
> - The vowels are *a, e, i, o,* and *u.*
> - Sometimes *y* is a vowel.
> - The rest of the letters are consonants.

1. A → E

  Ⓐ i → o   Ⓑ E → u   Ⓒ O → U   Ⓓ Y → y

2. e → s

  Ⓐ r → a   Ⓑ i → t   Ⓒ l → m   Ⓓ o → u

3. w → K

  Ⓐ a → F   Ⓑ P → j   Ⓒ i → E   Ⓓ d → H

4. Z → U

  Ⓐ G → E   Ⓑ i → o   Ⓒ S → T   Ⓓ A → C

5. b → v

  Ⓐ a → c   Ⓑ o → u   Ⓒ m → n   Ⓓ R → S

6. E → b

  Ⓐ U → c   Ⓑ X → t   Ⓒ a → E   Ⓓ M → y

Tell or Write: To answer the questions, was it important to . . .

- pay attention to vowels?   **yes**   **no**

- pay attention to upper and lower case?   **yes**   **no**

- pay attention to order?   **yes**   **no**

Writing Out the Link

Directions: Think about the link between the words. Write out how the words are tied together.

1. **cat : meow**   Meow is the sound a cat makes.

2. **chair : sit**

3. **ride : bike**

4. **bike : wheels**

5. **tame : wild**

6. **tire : rubber**

Writing Out the Link 2

Look at this word pair → | **owl : hoot** |

If you wrote how the words are linked, you might come up with

- An owl hoots.
- The sound an owl makes is a hoot.

Directions: Write down simple sentences or phrases to describe how the pairs are linked.

1. **foot : toes**

2. **fish : trout**

3. **go : stay**

4. **cook : stove**

5. **sister : brother**

6. **ruler : measure**

7. **cut : saw**

8. **yell : shout**

Keep this page! You will need your answers to use again.

Trying Out the Link

Directions: You will need your answers from the "Writing Out the Link 2" worksheet for this page.

| owl : hoot | → | An owl hoots.
The sound an owl makes. |

When you are trying to find a matching pair of words, try out the same link you used on the first pair. Does the phrase or sentence make sense?

Example: owl : hoot ➝ An owl hoots.

Ⓐ roar : lion ➝ A roar lions.

Ⓑ seal : bark ➝ A seal barks.

Fill in the circle next to the answer above that has the same link as **owl : hoot**.

Directions: Write out your link sentences with the words in these pairs. Mark the answer that fits.

Write Out

1. **foot : toes**   _____

Ⓐ   hand : fingers   _____

Ⓑ   ring : fingers   _____

2. **fish : trout**   _____

Ⓐ   shark : gill   _____

Ⓑ   flower : rose   _____

3. **go : stay**   _____

Ⓐ   win : lose   _____

Ⓑ   leave : exit   _____

Trying Out the Link 2

Directions: You will need your answers from the "Writing Out the Link 2" worksheet for this page. Write out your link sentences with the words in these pairs. Mark the answer that fits.

Write Out

4. **cook : stove**

   Ⓐ oven : hot

   Ⓑ sleep : bed

5. **sister : brother**

   Ⓐ mother : girl

   Ⓑ aunt : uncle

6. **ruler : measure**

   Ⓐ pen : write

   Ⓑ weigh : scale

7. **cut : saw**

   Ⓐ tear : rip

   Ⓑ sew : needle

8. **yell : shout**

   Ⓐ nap : sleep

   Ⓑ scream : sing

Writing a Linked Pair

Directions: Read the sentences below.

How do people stay cool? They sweat. People have sweat glands all over their bodies.

How do dogs and cats stay cool? Dogs and cats pant. Dogs and cats only have sweat glands on their feet.

How do birds stay cool? Birds pant. Birds do not have any sweat glands.

Directions: Use the information above to make your own linked pairs. Use the words from each word box.

---

cats   pant   sweat

1. **people :** _____ _____ _____ as _____ : _____

Write out the link sentence you used.

_____
_____
_____
_____
_____

---

glands   birds   people

2. **no sweat glands :** _____ _____ as _____ : _____

Write out the link sentence you used.

_____
_____
_____
_____

Writing a Linked Pair 2

Directions: Read the sentences below.

> The Fennec fox lives in Africa. It lives in the desert. The Fennec fox has large ears. It eats insects. The fox's large ears help it hear insects walking on the sand. Its ears help it stay cool, too.
>
> The African elephant lives in Africa. It is the largest land animal. It lives in grasslands. It eats grass and other plants. The African elephant has large ears. When it is hot, the elephant flaps it ears. It flaps it ears to cool down.

Directions: Use the information above to make your own linked pairs. Use the words from each word box.

> **grasslands   desert   elephant**

1. **fox :** ---------------------- as ------------------------------ : ----------------------

Write out the link sentence you used.

_____

- -

_____

_____

- -

_____

> **elephant   fox   plants**

2. **insects :** ---------------------- as ---------------------- : ---------------------------

Write out the link sentence you used.

_____

- -

_____

_____

- -

_____

Spelling

A **noun** is the name of a person, place, or thing. Here are some examples:

Person	Place	Thing
Tom	home	desk
mother	city	cup

Directions: Write down some other examples of nouns:

	Person	Place	Thing
1.			
2.			

When we make nouns plural (more than one), we have spelling rules.

Spelling Rule: If the word ends in *s, x, ch,* or *sh,* add *es* to the end.

Directions: Use the spelling rule to help you write in the correct answer.

1. **class : classes** *as* **grass :** _____

2. **box : boxes** *as* **fox :** _____

3. **bench : benches** *as* **stitch :** _____

4. **bush : bushes** *as* **wish :** _____

5. **bus : buses** *as* **lens :** _____

Spelling 2

Directions: Use this rule to help you find word pairs with the same link.

Spelling Rule: To make a noun that ends in *s, x, ch,* or *sh* plural, add *es* to the end.

1. **arch : arches**
- (A) dish : dishs
- (B) seat : seates
- (C) pass : passs
- (D) touch : touches

2. **dress : dresses**
- (A) ax : axs
- (B) itch : itches
- (C) moss : mossess
- (D) wrench : wrenchs

3. **marsh : marshes**
- (A) touch : touchs
- (B) kiss : kisss
- (C) sketch : sketches
- (D) dog : doges

4. **lunches : lunch**
- (A) fax : faxes
- (B) crash : crashes
- (C) dresses : dress
- (D) patch : patches

5. What was the link for Number 4?

_____

_____

6. Write your own. Use a noun and its plural. Give one right answer and two wrong ones.

(A) _____ : _____

(B) _____ : _____

(C) _____ : _____

What was the correct answer to your question and why?

_____

_____

_____

Verb Link

A **verb** is an action word. A verb tells what you are doing.

Examples: run, talk, think, sing

Directions: Write down two other examples of verbs.

_____   _____

-------------------------------   -------------------------------

_____   _____

A verb has tenses. It has a present tense. It has a past tense. Some word pairs are linked by verb tenses.

Directions: Find a word in the **Word Bank** to put in the empty box so the word pairs have the same link.

> ## Word Bank
>
> won   wins   caught   catching
>
> ran   running   drew   drawn

1.

| eat | : | ate | :: | win | : | |

2.

| buy | : | bought | :: | catch | : | |

3.

| sleep | : | slept | :: | run | : | |

4.

| grow | : | grew | :: | draw | : | |

5. Write out the word link between the pairs.

_____

_____
_____

_____

Verb Link 2

Directions: Choose the answer that shares the same link. (**Hint:** Watch for verb tenses!)

1. **sit : sat**

   (A) drink : drank

   (B) taught : teach

   (C) bitten : bite

   (D) broken : break

   Choose one of the wrong answers and explain why it is wrong.

   _____

   -

   _____

2. **pay : paid**

   (A) got : get

   (B) had : have

   (C) write : wrote

   (D) drank : drink

   Which answer for question 2 could be a correct answer for question 1?

   _____

   -

   _____

3. **fed : feed**

   (A) catch : caught

   (B) fly : flown

   (C) bend : bent

   (D) built : build

   Which answers for question 3 could be a correct answer for question 2?

   _____

   -

   _____

4. **brought : bring**

   (A) flee : fled

   (B) met : meet

   (C) freeze : frozen

   (D) make : made

   Which answer for question 4 could be a correct answer for question 3?

   _____

   -

   _____

What They Do

Directions: Find a word in the **Word Bank** to put in the empty box so the word pairs have the same link.

Word Bank

acts	dances	eats
flies	heals	hops
plays	races	sweeps

1. | teacher | : | teaches | :: | doctor | : | |

2. | artist | : | paints | :: | actor | : | |

3. | fish | : | swims | :: | bunny | : | |

4. | student | : | studies | :: | pilot | : | |

5. | fisherman | : | fishes | :: | race car driver | : | |

6. | singer | : | sings | :: | dancer | : | |

7. Write out the word link between the pairs.

_____

_____

_____

_____

8. Think of two words of your own that have the same link as above. Write them down.

| | : | |

What They Do 2

Directions: Choose the answer that shares the same link.

1. **whale : spouts**

   Ⓐ frog : flies   Ⓒ snake : runs

   Ⓑ penguin : swims   Ⓓ worm : hops

   Now fill in the words to complete the link sentences for question #1.

   yes or no

   - A w_____ s_____. _____yes_____
   - A f_____ f_____. _____
   - A p_____ s_____. _____
   - A s_____ r_____. _____
   - A w_____ h_____. _____

Directions: Choose the answer that shares the same link.

2. **storekeeper : sells**

   Ⓐ farmer : plants   Ⓒ bakes : baker

   Ⓑ sprays : firefighter   Ⓓ plays : musician

   Now complete the link sentences for question #2. Pay attention to what comes first!

   yes or no

   - A s_____ s_____. _____yes_____
   - A f_____ p_____. _____
   - A s_____ f_____. _____
   - A b_____ b_____. _____
   - A p_____ m_____. _____

Directions: Choose the answer that shares the same link

3. **sails : sailor**

   Ⓐ pencil : writer   Ⓒ explorer : explores

   Ⓑ paints : doctor   Ⓓ races : racer

   Which wrong answer for question 3 would be correct if the words were in a different order?

   _____

   _____

   _____

Purpose Link

Directions: Find a word in the **Word Bank** to put in the empty box so the word pairs have the same link.

Word Bank

ball	sweep	paint	ink
drive	burn	swing	read
page	inch	cool	write

1.

scissors	:	cut	::	book	:	

This can be read as *scissors* is to *cut* as *book* is to ----------------------------------- _____.

2.

shovel	:	dig	::	pen	:	

3.

knife	:	cut	::	bat	:	

4.

ruler	:	measure	::	car	:	

5.

scale	:	weigh	::	broom	:	

6.

heater	:	warm	::	fan	:	

7. Think of two words of your own that have the same link as above. Write them down.

	:	

Purpose Link 2

Directions: Fill in the words to complete the sentence for this link: | **ax : chop** |

1. You use an _____ to _____.

   Now choose the answer that shares the same link.

   | **ax : chop** |

   Ⓐ knife : sharp   Ⓒ brush : paint

   Ⓑ color : red   Ⓓ table : plate

Directions: Fill in the words to complete two sentences for this link: | **bed : sleep** |.

2. You _____ in a _____. You use a _____ to _____.

   Now choose the answer that shares the same link.

   | **bed : sleep** |

   Ⓐ eat : fork   Ⓒ wall : window

   Ⓑ oven : kitchen   Ⓓ chair : sit

Directions: Choose the answer that shares the same link.

3. **Ax** is to **chop** as **saw** is to _____.

   Ⓐ tree   Ⓑ cut   Ⓒ teeth   Ⓓ sharp

4. **Bed** is to **sleep** as **tub** is to _____.

   Ⓐ bathe   Ⓑ water   Ⓒ sink   Ⓓ hot

Directions: Use this fun fact to answer the question: *A snake uses its tongue to smell.*

5. **snake tongue : smell**

   Ⓐ see : person eye   Ⓒ person nose : feel

   Ⓑ taste : person tongue   Ⓓ person ear : hear

Part to Whole

Directions: Find a word in the **Word Bank** to put in the empty box so the word pairs have the same link.

Word Bank

alphabet	door	forest	minute
book	wall	hand	year
city	foot	letter	

1. | day | : | week | :: | month | : | |

2. | room | : | house | :: | brick | : | |

3. | word | : | sentence | :: | page | : | |

4. | branch | : | tree | :: | toe | : | |

5. | wall | : | room | :: | tree | : | |

6. | hour | : | day | :: | letter | : | |

7. Write out the word link between the pairs.

_____

- -

_____

- -

_____

8. Think of two words of your own that have the same link. Write them down.

| | : | |

Part to Whole 2

Directions: Look at the pictures. Choose the answer that makes the best link.

1.

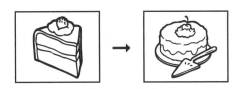

   Ⓐ **good** to **bad**   Ⓒ **bad** to **good**

   Ⓑ **all** to **part**   Ⓓ **part** to **all**

Directions: Look at the word and picture pairs below. Choose the pair that has the same link as the pictures in question 1. If no pairs have the same link, fill in answer choice "c."

2.

      Ⓐ   Ⓑ   Ⓒ

c ➡ cat   cat ➡ c   no same link

3.

      Ⓐ   Ⓑ   Ⓒ

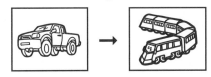   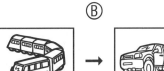   no same link

4.

      Ⓐ   Ⓑ   Ⓒ

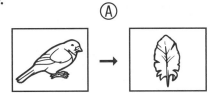   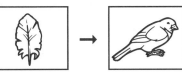   no same link

5.

      Ⓐ   Ⓑ   Ⓒ

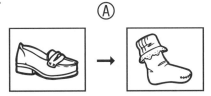   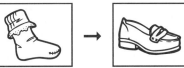   no same link

6.

      Ⓐ   Ⓑ   Ⓒ

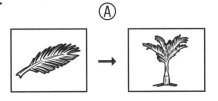   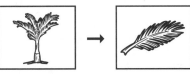   no same link

Use What You Know

Sometimes you may not know a word. Don't give up! Sometimes you can figure out the answer by using what you know.

Directions: Read all of the answer choices. Cross out the ones that you know are wrong. You will know they are not correct because they do not have the same link. Choose the answer that is left.

(**Hint:** In your head, read question #1 as "**Dog** is to **puppy** as _____ is to _____.")

1. **dog : puppy**
   - (A) rat : tail
   - (B) cow : milk
   - (C) cat : meow
   - (D) kangaroo : joey

2. **small : tiny**
   - (A) old : young
   - (B) sweet : sour
   - (C) big : immense
   - (D) wrong : right

3. **strong : weak**
   - (A) super : great
   - (B) glad : miserable
   - (C) sleepy : tired
   - (D) cheerful : happy

4. **lion : mammal**
   - (A) sloth : mammal
   - (B) frog: mammal
   - (C) snake : mammal
   - (D) dinosaur : mammal

Directions: Use what you know to complete the following sentences.

5. Most likely, a joey is a _____ .

6. Most likely, when something is immense, it is very _____ .

7. Most likely, if someone is miserable, he or she is not _____ .

8. Most likely, a _____ is a type of mammal.

Use What You Know 2

Directions: Read all of the answer choices. Cross out the ones that you know are wrong. You will know they are not correct because they do not have the same link. Choose the answer that is left.

1. **deer : fawn**

- Ⓐ cow : milk
- Ⓑ swan : cygnet
- Ⓒ chick : rooster
- Ⓓ kitten : purr

2. **hot : cold**

- Ⓐ vast : tiny
- Ⓑ wrong : incorrect
- Ⓒ happy : cheerful
- Ⓓ sleepy : tired

3. **big : large**

- Ⓐ soft : hard
- Ⓑ small : giant
- Ⓒ happy : sad
- Ⓓ silly : ridiculous

4. **robin : bird**

- Ⓐ flower : lizard
- Ⓑ blue whale : lizard
- Ⓒ komodo dragon : lizard
- Ⓓ snake : lizard

Directions: Now use what you know to complete the following sentences.

5. Most likely, a cygnet is a _____ .

6. Most likely, when something is silly, it is _____ .

7. Most likely, if something is vast, it is not _____ .

8. Most likely, a _____ is a type of lizard.

Use What You Know 3

Directions: Read the answer choices. Think about how the words are linked. Choose the pair of words that is *not* linked in the same way as the others. **If the words are linked in the same way, they cannot be the answer!** There is only one correct answer.

1. Ⓐ open : shut   Ⓒ big : large

   Ⓑ in : out   Ⓓ go : stop

   Wrong choices: _____, _____, _____

   Answer that must be right: _____

2. Ⓐ ears : hear   Ⓒ eyes : see

   Ⓑ leg : knee   Ⓓ nose : smell

   Wrong choices: _____, _____, _____

   Answer that must be right: _____

3. **boomer : kangaroo**

   Ⓐ buck : deer   Ⓒ cat : kitten

   Ⓑ dog : puppy   Ⓓ duck : duckling

   Wrong choices: _____, _____, _____

   Answer that must be right: _____

4. **broccoli : vegetable**

   Ⓐ apple : green   Ⓒ strawberry : red

   Ⓑ banana : yellow   Ⓓ peach : fruit

   Wrong choices: _____, _____, _____

   Answer that must be right: _____

Directions: Now use what you know to complete the following sentences.

5. Most likely, a male kangaroo is called a _____ .

6. Most likely, broccoli is a kind of _____ .

Tell or Write: Write down four pairs of answer choices. Make three of them the same link. See if a classmate can tell you which one is not linked in the same way.

Ⓐ _____ _____ : _____ _____

Ⓑ _____ _____ : _____ _____

Ⓒ _____ _____ : _____ _____

Ⓓ _____ _____ : _____ _____

Use What You Know 4

Directions: Read the answer choices. Think about how the words are linked. Choose the pair of words that is *not* linked in the same way as the others. **If the words are linked in the same way, they cannot be the answer!** There is only one correct answer.

1. (A) hurry : rush   (C) nap : sleep

 (B) run : crawl   (D) buy : shop

Wrong choices: _____, _____, _____

Answer that must be right: _____

2. (A) nail : hammer   (C) sew : needle

 (B) screw : screwdriver (D) branch : tree

Wrong choices: _____, _____, _____

Answer that must be right: _____

3. **xenopus : frog**

 (A) oak : tree   (C) exit : enter

 (B) up : down   (D) start : end

Wrong choices: _____, _____, _____

Answer that must be right: _____

4. **massive : big**

 (A) bunny : hops   (C) little : small

 (B) bird : flies   (D) whale : swims

Wrong choices: _____, _____, _____

Answer that must be right: _____

Directions: Now use what you know to complete the following sentences.

5. Most likely, a xenopus is a kind of _____ .

6. Most likely, something massive is _____ .

Tell or Write: Write down four pairs of answer choices. Make three of them the same link. See if a classmate can tell you which one is not linked in the same way.

(A) _____ : _____

(C) _____ : _____

(B) _____ : _____

(D) _____ : _____

Practice What You Know

Directions: Choose the answer that has the same link as the word pair. Pay attention to spelling and word order.

1. **box : boxes**

(A) crashes : crash

(B) tax : taxs

(C) match : matches

(D) marsh : marshs

2. **few : many**

(A) quick : fast

(B) cold : hot

(C) smart : wise

(D) pretty : beautiful

3. **buy : bought**

(A) swam : swim

(B) grew : grow

(C) caught : catch

(D) write : wrote

4. **tail : wag**

(A) eye : see

(B) smell : nose

(C) hear : ear

(D) teeth : lip

5. **boat : floats**

(A) rabbit : flies

(B) fish : swims

(C) jumps : frog

(D) plane : twirls

6. **stop : halt**

(A) far : near

(B) top : bottom

(C) high : low

(D) shut : close

7. **fingers : ten**

(A) ten : toes

(B) one : nose

(C) eyes : two

(D) fingers : toes

8. **fast : slow**

(A) young : old

(B) cold : freezing

(C) walk : fast

(D) slow : jog

Link Review

Directions: Draw lines to match the word pairs on the left with the type of link on the right.

1. <u>kitten</u> to <u>cat</u>

A. antonym (opposite meaning)

2. <u>petal</u> to <u>flower</u>

B. synonym (same meaning)

3. <u>pen</u> to <u>write</u>

C. homophone (same sound)

4. <u>large</u> to <u>big</u>

D. part to whole

5. <u>bench</u> to <u>benches</u>

E. whole to part

6. <u>ocean</u> to <u>pond</u>

F. one to more (plural)

7. <u>hot</u> to <u>cold</u>

G. more (plural) to one

8. <u>house</u> to <u>room</u>

H. big to small

9. <u>geese</u> to <u>goose</u>

I. small to big

10. <u>ate</u> to <u>eight</u>

J. purpose

Link Review 2

Directions: Draw lines to match the word pairs on the left with the type of link on the right.

1. <u>mountain</u> to <u>hill</u>

2. <u>tell</u> to <u>told</u>

3. <u>page</u> to <u>book</u>

4. <u>flour</u> to <u>flower</u>

5. <u>shirt</u> to <u>sleeve</u>

6. <u>girl</u> to <u>woman</u>

7. <u>quiet</u> to <u>loud</u>

8. <u>rope</u> to <u>tie</u>

9. <u>fast</u> to <u>quick</u>

10. <u>shook</u> to <u>shake</u>

A. antonym (opposite meaning)

B. synonym (same meaning)

C. homophone (same sound)

D. part to whole

E. whole to part

F. past tense to present tense

G. present tense to past tense

H. big to small

I. small to big

J. purpose

Practice Being the Teacher

Directions: It is your turn to teach. Look at the word pair in the box. Show how to find the answer by completing the questions that follow.

fox : animal

(A) first : last   (C) dandelion : plant

(B) empty : full   (D) bird : woodpecker

1. First, make your link sentence.

   • A _____ is a kind of _____.

   Next, try out the link by writing in the word pairs:

   • A ___f_____ is a kind of ___l_____.

   • An ___e_____ is a kind of ___f_____.

   • A ___d_____ is a kind of ___p_____.

   • A ___b_____ is a kind of ___w_____.

2. Answers _____ and _____ cannot be right because they have the same link. They are both_____.

3. Answer _____ cannot be right because it is in the wrong order.

---

4. Choose what the answer would be if the question was | **foxes : animal** | .

   (A) dandelion : plant   (C) dandelions : plant

   (B) dandelion : plants   (D) dandelions : plants

5. Answers _____ and _____ are wrong because there should be more than one dandelion.

6. Answer _____ is wrong because there should be only one plant.

Practice Being the Teacher 2

Directions: It is your turn to teach. Look at the word pair below. Show how to find the answer by completing the questions that follow.

blink : eye

    (A) hand : wave   (C) wag : tail

    (B) shoe : foot   (D) hat : head

1. First, make your link sentence.

- You _____ an _____ .

Next, try out the link by writing in the word pairs:

- You ___h_____ a ___w_____.

- You _____ a _____.

- You _____ a _____.

- You _____ a _____.

2. Answers _____ and _____ cannot be right because they have the same link.

3. Answers _____ cannot be right because it is in the wrong order.

4. Choose what the answer would be if the question was   **arms : starfish** .

    (A) petal : flower   (C) petals : flower

    (B) petal : flowers   (D) petals : flowers

5. Answers _____ and _____ are wrong because there should be more than one petal.

6. Answer _____ is wrong because there should be only one flower.

Answer Sheets

These sheets may be used to provide practice in answering questions in a standardized-test format.

Student's Name: _____

_____

Activity Page: _____

1. Ⓐ   Ⓑ   Ⓒ   Ⓓ

2. Ⓐ   Ⓑ   Ⓒ   Ⓓ

3. Ⓐ   Ⓑ   Ⓒ   Ⓓ

4. Ⓐ   Ⓑ   Ⓒ   Ⓓ

5. Ⓐ   Ⓑ   Ⓒ   Ⓓ

6. Ⓐ   Ⓑ   Ⓒ   Ⓓ

7. Ⓐ   Ⓑ   Ⓒ   Ⓓ

8. Ⓐ   Ⓑ   Ⓒ   Ⓓ

9. Ⓐ   Ⓑ   Ⓒ   Ⓓ

10. Ⓐ   Ⓑ   Ⓒ   Ⓓ

Student's Name: _____

_____

Activity Page: _____

1. Ⓐ   Ⓑ   Ⓒ   Ⓓ

2. Ⓐ   Ⓑ   Ⓒ   Ⓓ

3. Ⓐ   Ⓑ   Ⓒ   Ⓓ

4. Ⓐ   Ⓑ   Ⓒ   Ⓓ

5. Ⓐ   Ⓑ   Ⓒ   Ⓓ

6. Ⓐ   Ⓑ   Ⓒ   Ⓓ

7. Ⓐ   Ⓑ   Ⓒ   Ⓓ

8. Ⓐ   Ⓑ   Ⓒ   Ⓓ

9. Ⓐ   Ⓑ   Ⓒ   Ⓓ

10. Ⓐ   Ⓑ   Ⓒ   Ⓓ

Answer Key

Fitting Pictures Together (page 4)

1. dog (not cat)
2. little dog (not big)
3. sandal (not covered)
4. soft chair (has cushion)
5. snake (doesn't fly)
6. tennis racquet (not ball)

Fitting Pictures Together 2 (page 5)

1. carrot (not fruit)
2. T (not lowercase)
3. rectangle (not square)
4. brush (not instrument)
5. butterfly (not bird)

Fitting Pictures Together 3 (page 6)

1. apple (only fruit, no bread)
2. kitten (not dinosaur)
3. kite (doesn't have to do with space)
4. refrigerator (can't carry)
5. spider (has eight legs)
6. dog (doesn't lay eggs)

Linking Pictures (page 7)

1. A   4. A
2. C   5. A
3. B   6. C

Linking Pictures 2 (page 8)

1. B
2. A
3. C
4. C
5. B
6. Answers will vary.

Linking Pictures 3 (page 9)

1. C   4. A
2. B   5. B
3. C   6. A

The Same Link (page 10)

1. C   3. D
2. A   4. B

The Same Link 2 (page 11)

1. B
2. C
3. C
4. A
5. Answers will vary.

Paying Attention (page 12)

1. A   3. C
2. C   4. A

Paying Attention 2 (page 13)

1. A   3. C
2. C   4. B

Things that Go Together (page 14)

1. B   4. C
2. D   5. D
3. A   6. A

Matching Linking Pairs (page 15)

Accept appropriate pairings.

Matching Linking Pairs 2 (page 16)

Accept appropriate pairings.

Body Parts (page 17)

1. A
2. C
3. B
4. B
5. The number "8" should be one of the answers.

Color (page 18)

1. B
2. C
3. C
4. A
5. The color "red" should be one of the answers.

Math (page 19)

1. B   4. A
2. C   5. B
3. C   6. A

Math 2 (page 20)

1. C
2. C
3. B
4. C
5. The number "3" should be one of the answers.

Math 3 (page 21)

1. A
2. C
3. B
4. A
5. reverse order of one

Social Studies (page 22)

1. C   4. B
2. A   5. A
3. B

Social Studies 2 (page 23)

1. A   3. C
2. B   4. B

Time (page 24)

1. B   3. B
2. B   4. C

Time 2 (page 25)

1. C   3. A
2. B   4. A

Science (page 26)

1. B
2. C
3. A
4. A bird should be one of the answers.

Science 2 (page 27)

1. C   3. B
2. A   4. C

Answer Key (cont.)

The Solar System (page 28)

1. C   4. D
2. B   5. A
3. B

The Solar System 2 (page 29)

1. D   4. C
2. D   5. B
3. A

Antonyms (page 30)

1. C, small
2. B, happy
3. A, short
4. A, young
5. C, asleep
6. B, few
7. C, under
8. A, out
9. C, fast
10. B, far

Synonyms (page 31)

1. B, tiny
2. C, large
3. A, catch
4. A, grin
5. C, quick
6. B, weep
7. B, shout
8. C, exit
9. A, close
10. C, funny

Antonym and Synonym Practice (page 32)

1. B, A   4. A, A
2. D, A   5. B, S
3. C, S   6. D, S

Words that Sound the Same (page 33)

1. B (bee, two)
2. D (knight, tail)
3. A (hare, eight)
4. C (flower, road)

Alphabet Practice (page 34)

1. A   4. B
2. C   5. D
3. D   6. C

Alphabet Practice 2 (page 35)

1. C   4. A
2. B   5. C
3. D   6. A

Writing Out the Link (page 36)

2. You sit on a chair; a chair is to sit on.
3. You ride a bike; a bike is to ride.
4. A bike has wheels.
5. If it's tame, it's not wild. (opposites or antonyms)
6. A tire is made of rubber.

Writing Out the Link 2 (page 37)

Answers will vary.

1. five toes on a foot
2. trout is a type of fish
3. opposites (antonyms)
4. use a stove to cook
5. girl and boy
6. use a ruler to measure
7. cut with a saw
8. synonyms

Trying Out the Link (page 38)

1. A
2. B
3. A

Trying Out the Link 2 (page 39)

4. B
5. B
6. A
7. B
8. A

Writing a Linked Pair (page 40)

1. <u>people : sweat</u> as <u>cats : pant</u>; People sweat to stay cool, as cats pant to stay cool.
2. <u>no sweat glands : birds</u> as <u>glands : people</u> ; number of sweat glands in animal

Writing a Linked Pair 2 (page 41)

1. <u>fox : desert</u> as <u>elephant : grasslands</u>; or, <u>fox : elephant</u> as <u>desert : grasslands</u>. The link is "where the animal lives."
2. <u>insects : fox</u> as <u>plants : elephant</u>; or <u>insects : plants</u> as <u>fox : elephant</u>. The link is "what the animal eats."

Spelling (page 42)

1. grasses
2. foxes
3. stitches
4. wishes
5. lenses

Spelling 2 (page 43)

1. D
2. B
3. C
4. C
5. plural to singular

Verb Link (page 44)

1. won
2. caught
3. ran
4. drew
5. present to past verb tense

Answer Key *(cont.)*

Verb Link 2 (page 45)
1. A; Answers will vary.
2. C; C
3. D; A, B, C
4. B; B

What They Do (page 46)
1. heals
2. acts
3. hops
4. flies
5. races
6. dances
7. name of something to what it does

What They Do 2 (page 47)
1. B
2. A
3. D; C

Purpose Link (page 48)
1. read
2. write
3. swing
4. drive
5. sweep
6. cool

Purpose Link 2 (page 49)
1. C
2. D
3. B
4. A
5. D

Part to Whole (page 50)
1. year
2. wall
3. book
4. foot
5. forest
6. alphabet
7. link is "part to whole"

Part to Whole 2 (page 51)
1. D
2. A
3. C
4. B
5. C
6. A

Use What You Know (page 52)
1. D
2. C
3. B
4. A
5. baby kangaroo
6. big
7. glad
8. sloth

Use What You Know 2 (page 53)
1. B
2. A
3. D
4. C
5. baby swan
6. ridiculous
7. tiny
8. komodo dragon

Use What You Know 3 (page 54)
1. wrong: A, B, D; right: C
2. wrong: A, C, D; right: B
3. wrong: B, C, D; right: A
4. wrong: A, B, C; right: D
5. boomer
6. vegetable

Use What You Know 4 (page 55)
1. wrong: A, C, D; right: B
2. wrong: A, B, C; right: D
3. wrong: B, C, D; right: A
4. wrong: A, B, D; right: C
5. frog
6. big

Practice What You Know (page 56)
1. C
2. B
3. D
4. A
5. B
6. D
7. C
8. A

Link Review (page 57)
1. I
2. D
3. J
4. B
5. F
6. H
7. A
8. E
9. G
10. C

Link Review 2 (page 58)
1. H
2. G
3. D
4. C
5. E
6. I
7. A
8. J
9. B
10. F

Practice Being the Teacher (page 59)
1. A fox is a kind of animal.
2. A and B; opposites
3. D
4. C
5. A and B
6. D

Practice Being the Teacher 2 (page 60)
1. You blink an eye.
2. B and D
3. A
4. C
5. A and B
6. D